WORLD ABOUT US
POLLUTING THE OCEANS

M. BRIGHT

Central Rappahannock Regional Library
1201 Caroline Street
Fredericksburg, VA 22401

GLOUCESTER PRESS
London·New York·Toronto·Sydney

© Aladdin Books Ltd. 1991

First published in
the United States in 1991 by
Gloucester Press
387 Park Avenue South
New York NY 10016

Design: David West
Children's
Book Design
Editor: Fiona Robertson
Illustrator: James Macdonald
Consultant: Gail Bowering

Library of Congress
Cataloging-in-Publication Data

Bright, Michael.
Polluting the oceans / Michael
Bright.
p.cm. -- (World about us)
Includes index.
Summary: Examines the effects
of pollutants on the sea and
marine life and efforts to clean
up the waters and prevent
further damage.
ISBN 0-531-17353-4
1. Marine pollution--Juvenile
literature. [1. Marine pollution.
2. Pollution.] I. Title. II. Series.
GC1085.B75   1991
363.73'94'09162--dc20
91-11580   CIP   AC

Printed in Belgium
All rights reserved

J
363.73
Br
c.2

Contents

Ocean life
4
Natural controls
6
The coral reefs
8
Chemical pollution
10
Farm poisons
12
The ocean dump
14
Oil pollution
16
Waste for ever
18
Causing disease
20
Hotspots
22
Cleaning up
24
Taking action
26
Did you know?
28
Glossary
31
Index
32

Introduction

The oceans cover three-quarters of the earth. They play a vital part in controlling the world's weather. For centuries, they have provided people with a source of food and water, and with a way of transporting goods, and discovering new lands. Now, however, the oceans are being increasingly exploited. As the population goes up, so does the amount of poisonous wastes found in the sea. This has led to very high levels of pollution in some areas.

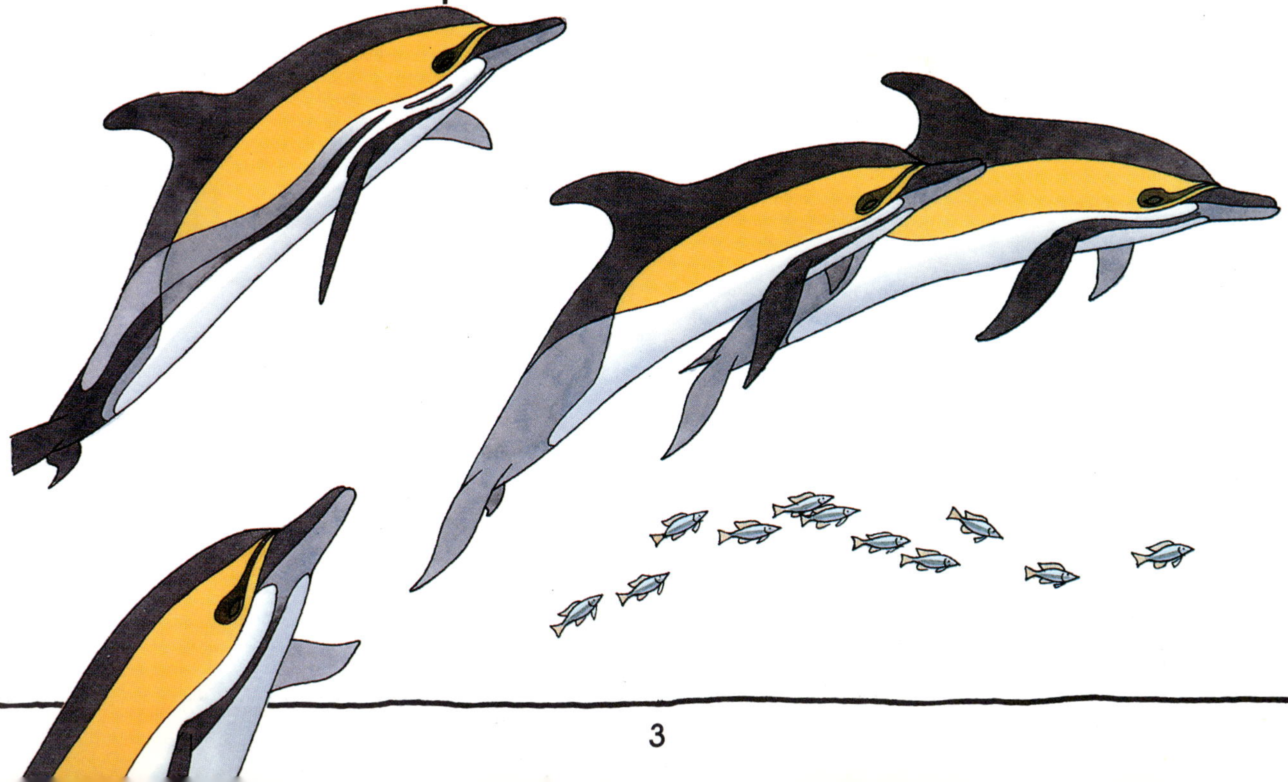

Ocean life

The oceans contain a wonderful variety of life. Creatures too small to be seen with the unaided eye, called plant plankton, live on the surface. Beneath the waves, fish of every size and shape can be found, like the brightly colored parrot fish, or enormous fish like tuna. Some mammals also live in the sea, like whales, dolphins, and seals. Seabirds dive into the waves looking for food.

A food chain is formed when large animals feed on smaller ones. In the sea, animal and plant plankton are at the bottom of the food chain. All living things depend on food chains to survive.

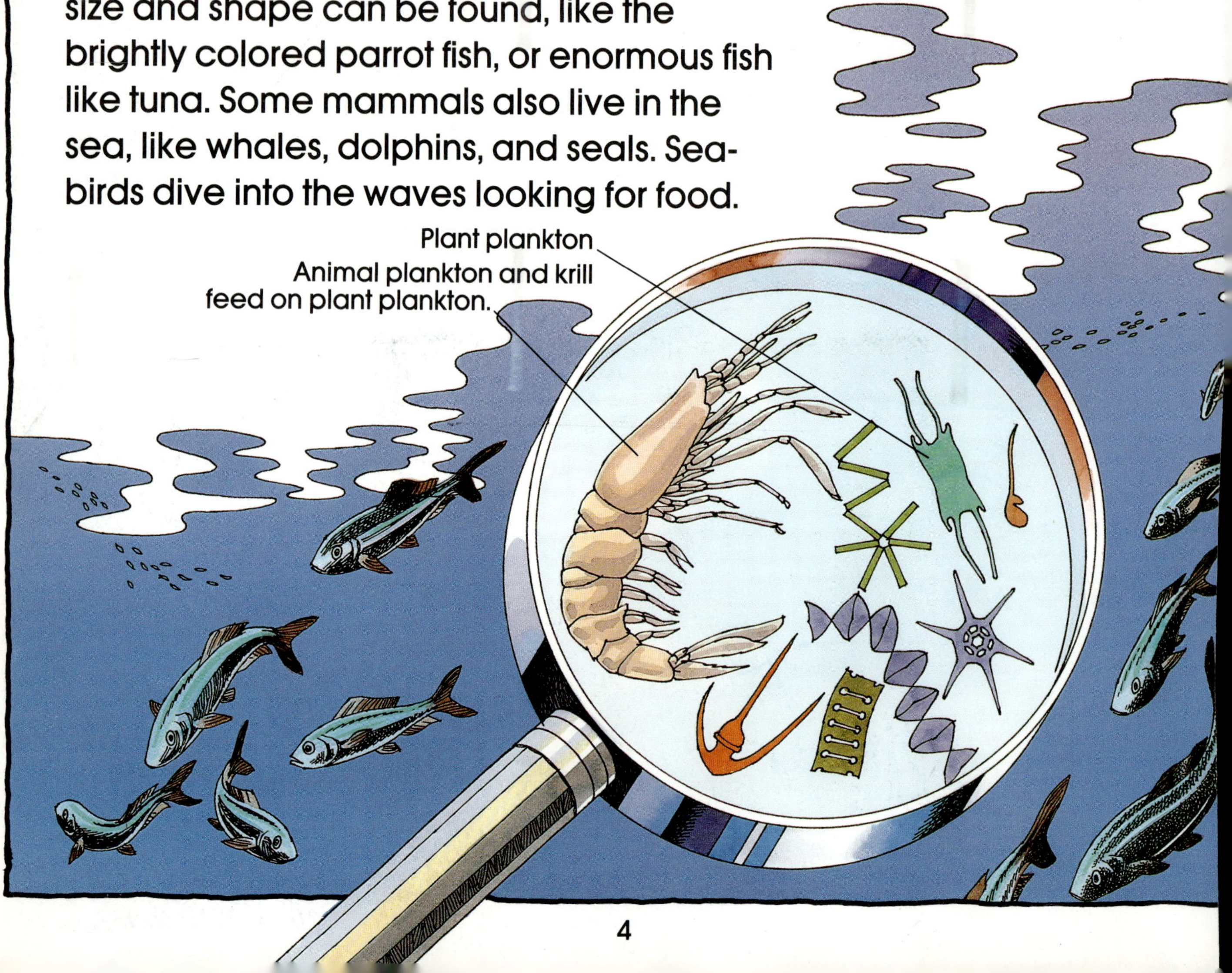

Plant plankton
Animal plankton and krill feed on plant plankton.

Land and sea
The seas contain over 90 percent of the world's water. Water vapor from the sea makes clouds form, which blow across the land, bringing rain.

Volcanoes produce dust, ash and gases, all of which can get into the sea. They are carried there by rivers, by the wind, or in rain.

Natural controls

Substances like oil and sulfur are found leaking naturally into the ocean through cracks in the ocean floor. Dust from volcanoes contains tiny specks of metals which are blown across the seas. In most cases, the sea can deal with the amounts produced of such substances. But large amounts of polluting substances are now leaked or dumped in the sea, and this natural system can no longer cope.

Certain types of bacteria break down the naturally-produced oil and sulfur. They are eaten by creatures like crabs and mussels, many of which are huge, like clams 16 inches across.

Naturally leaking oil and sulfur

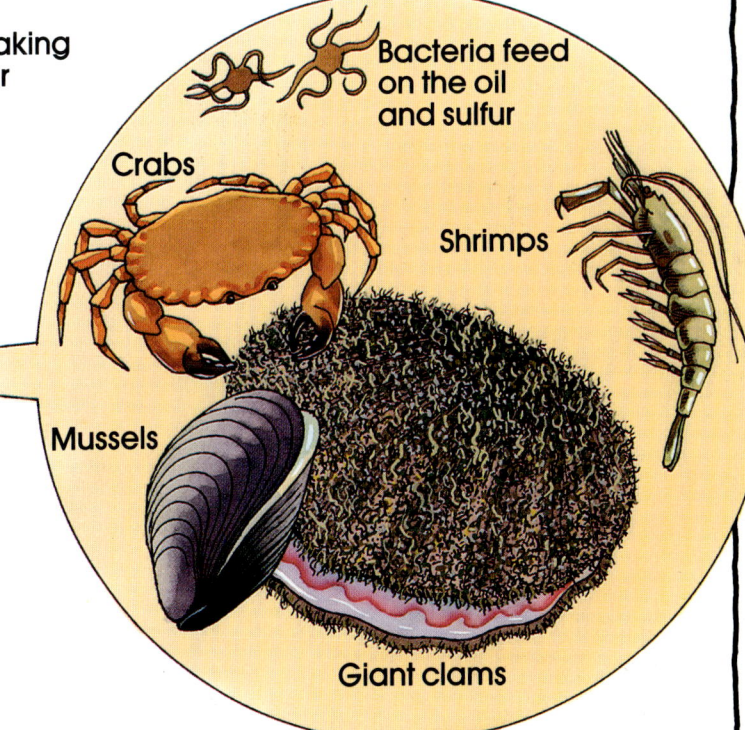

Bacteria feed on the oil and sulfur
Crabs
Shrimps
Mussels
Giant clams

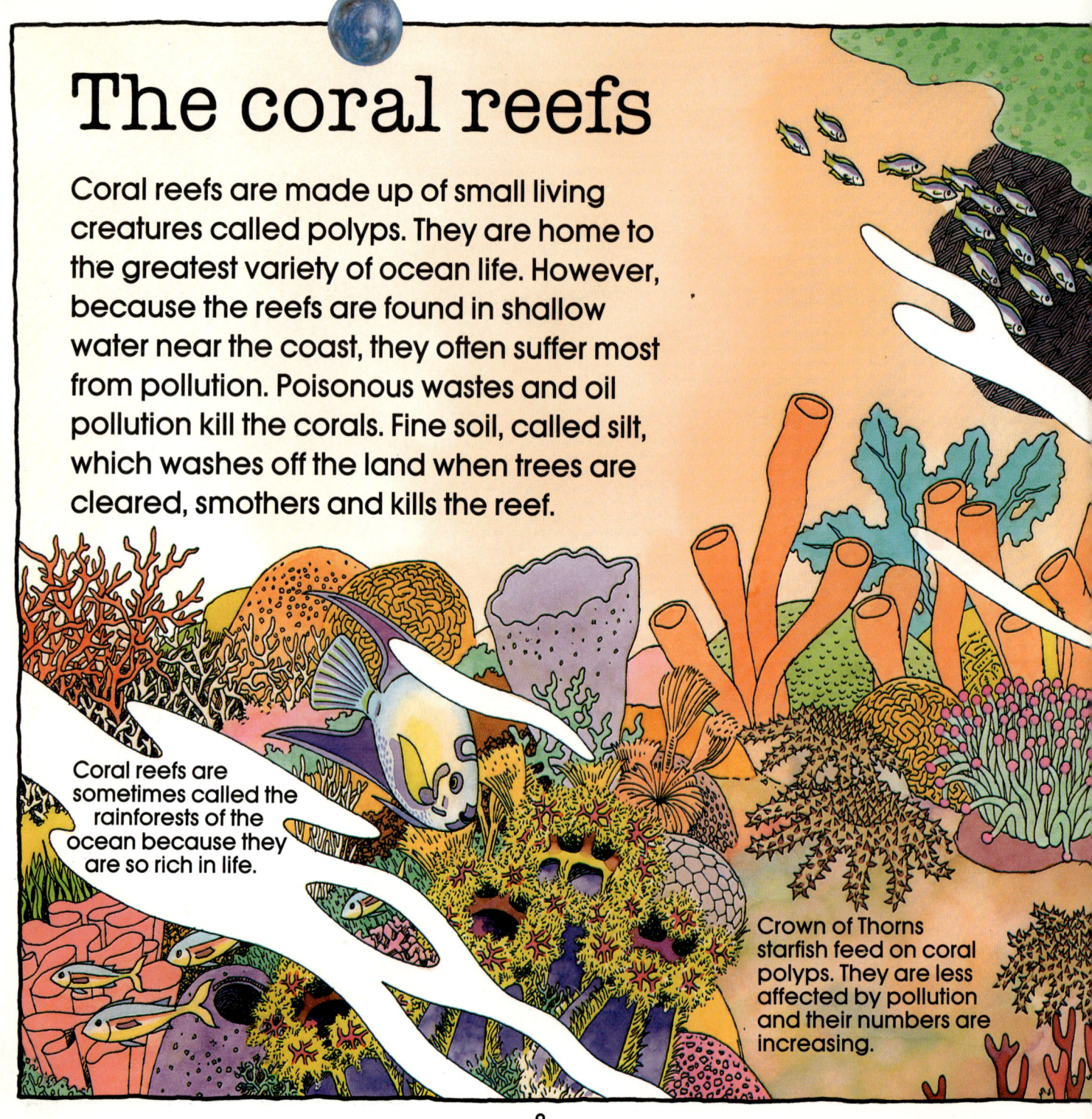

The coral reefs

Coral reefs are made up of small living creatures called polyps. They are home to the greatest variety of ocean life. However, because the reefs are found in shallow water near the coast, they often suffer most from pollution. Poisonous wastes and oil pollution kill the corals. Fine soil, called silt, which washes off the land when trees are cleared, smothers and kills the reef.

Coral reefs are sometimes called the rainforests of the ocean because they are so rich in life.

Crown of Thorns starfish feed on coral polyps. They are less affected by pollution and their numbers are increasing.

Chemical pollution

Chemical wastes from factories can end up in the sea, often carried there by rivers. Some of these wastes are lethal. In 1986 a fire broke out at a chemical factory on the Rhine River. So much pollution was released that for 90 miles of the river all life was killed. Other types of chemical waste are not easily broken down. They build up inside animals' bodies and stay in the food chain for years.

Many factories are built along the shoreline of rivers, lakes, and oceans because huge amounts of water are used in industry.

Untreated sewage and chemical wastes are often pumped directly into the river or ocean.

The beluga, or white whale, lives in the Arctic. It is being affected by pollution from the St. Lawrence River in Canada. Many are dying or can no longer reproduce.

Pole to Pole
Pollutants from North America are carried to the Arctic in ocean currents. Polar bears there have high levels of pollutants in their bodies.

In the Antarctic, large amounts of pesticide have been found in penguins and their eggs. Yet in both of these polar areas, the nearest factory is many miles away.

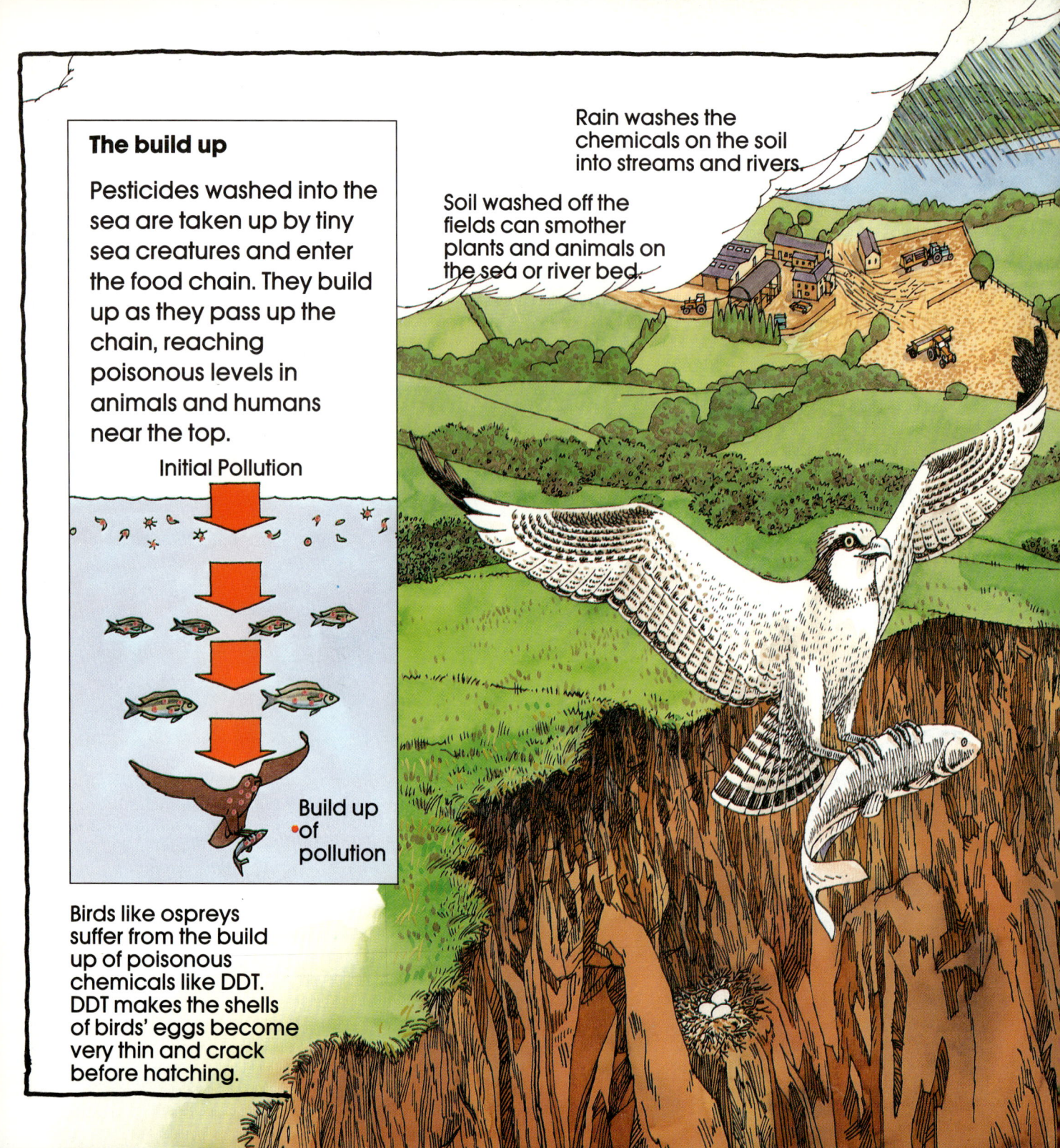

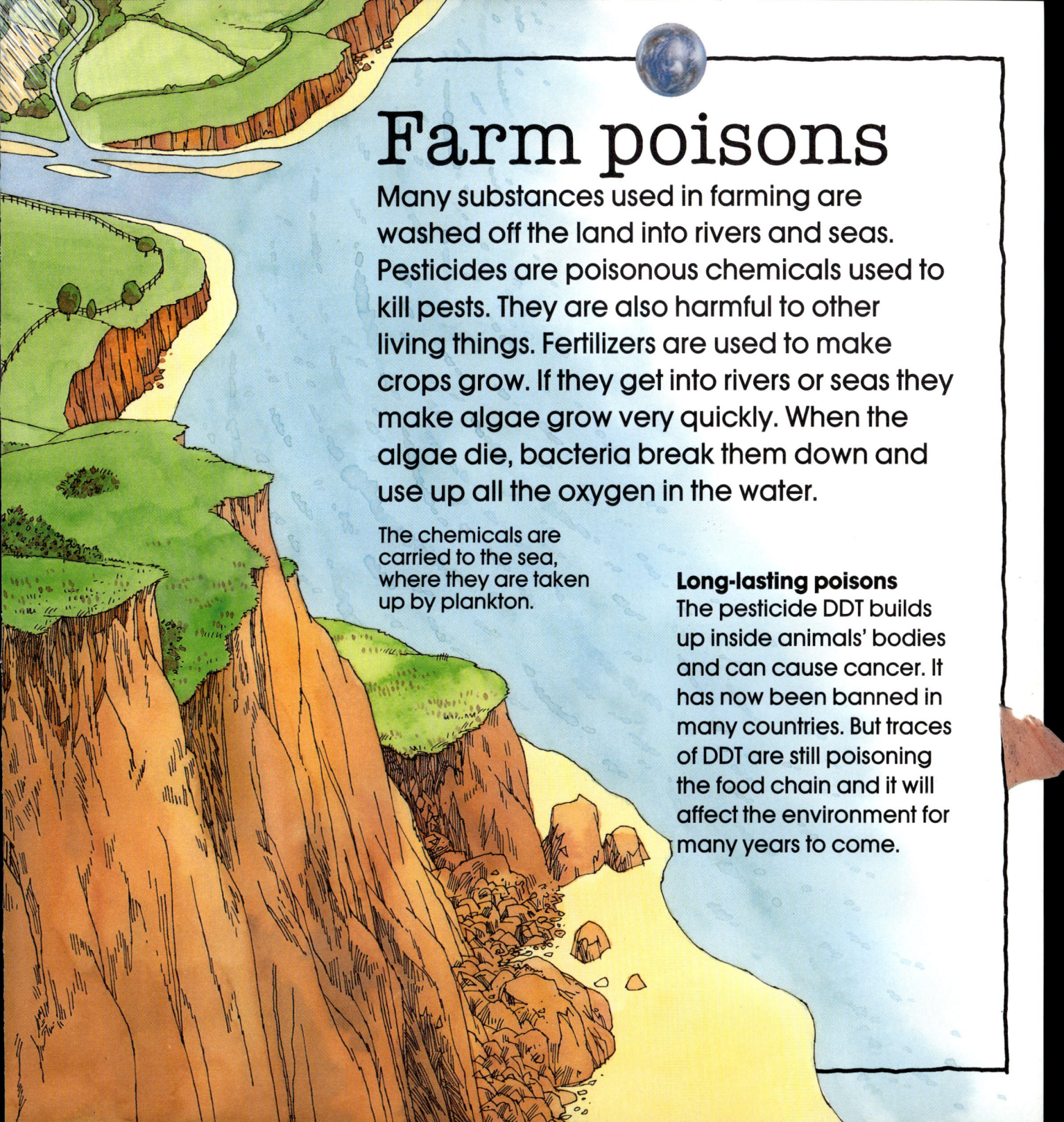

Farm poisons

Many substances used in farming are washed off the land into rivers and seas. Pesticides are poisonous chemicals used to kill pests. They are also harmful to other living things. Fertilizers are used to make crops grow. If they get into rivers or seas they make algae grow very quickly. When the algae die, bacteria break them down and use up all the oxygen in the water.

The chemicals are carried to the sea, where they are taken up by plankton.

Long-lasting poisons
The pesticide DDT builds up inside animals' bodies and can cause cancer. It has now been banned in many countries. But traces of DDT are still poisoning the food chain and it will affect the environment for many years to come.

Many types of pollution cannot be seen. People may swim in water, not knowing it is polluted.

Waste burned at sea in incinerator ships releases tiny amounts of poisonous unburned chemicals into the sea.

Arctic Rubbish
The sharp edges of old tin cans and broken bottles can seriously injure animals like this polar bear, looking for food in the garbage thrown away by explorers or washed up by the sea.

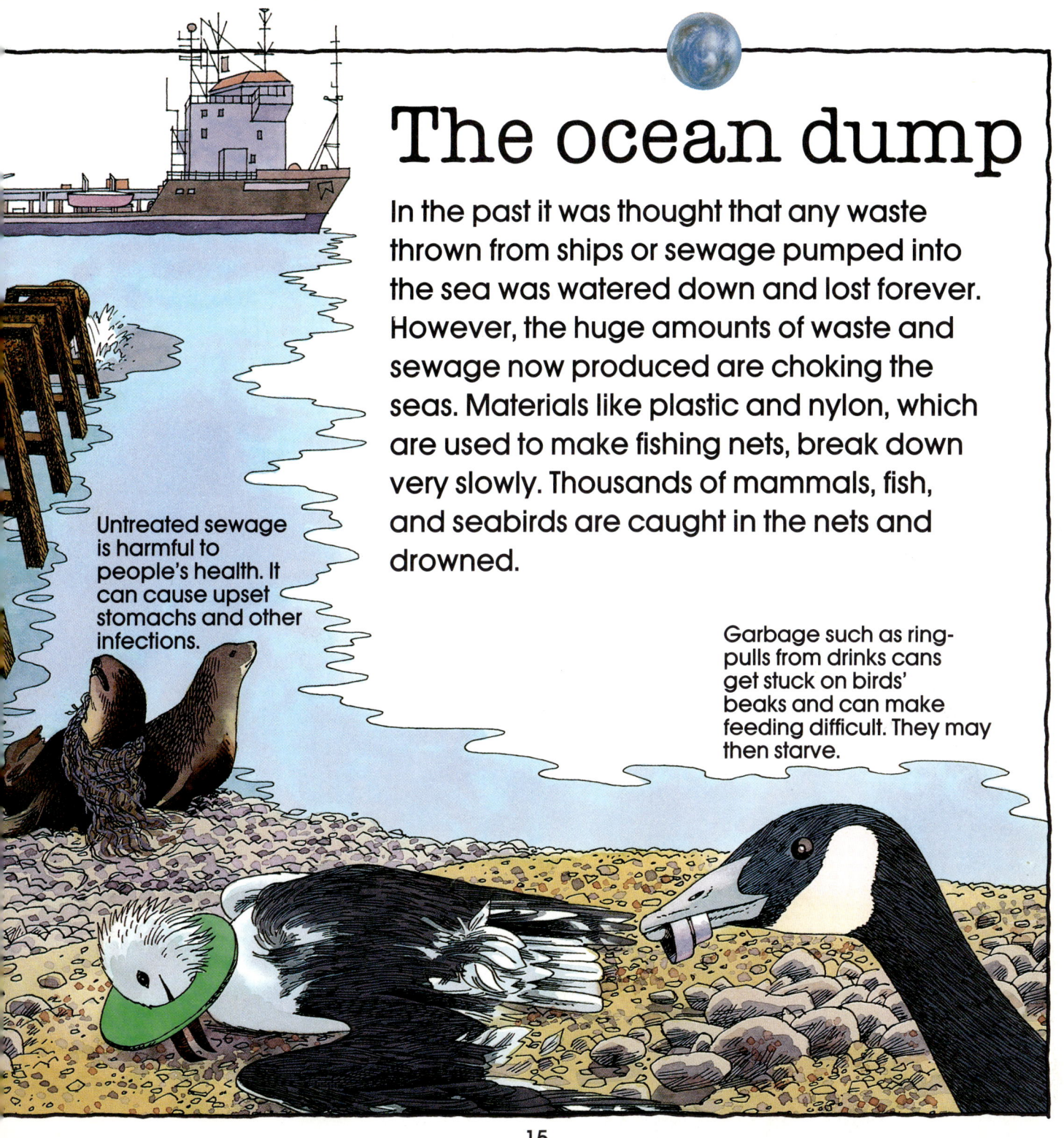

The ocean dump

In the past it was thought that any waste thrown from ships or sewage pumped into the sea was watered down and lost forever. However, the huge amounts of waste and sewage now produced are choking the seas. Materials like plastic and nylon, which are used to make fishing nets, break down very slowly. Thousands of mammals, fish, and seabirds are caught in the nets and drowned.

Untreated sewage is harmful to people's health. It can cause upset stomachs and other infections.

Garbage such as ring-pulls from drinks cans get stuck on birds' beaks and can make feeding difficult. They may then starve.

Oil pollution

Only a tiny amount of oil pollution comes from wrecked tankers. The major causes are tankers washing out their tanks with seawater, accidents on drilling platforms and leaks from pipelines under the sea. Oil slicks kill hundreds of seabirds, fish, and shellfish, and have serious results for local people. Their food source is poisoned and many fishermen lose their jobs.

11 million gallons of oil were spilled when the oil tanker *Exxon Valdez* ran aground in Alaska. Thousands of fish, birds, and other sea creatures were killed. Exxon has to pay $5 billion for the devastation caused, plus the costs of cleaning up the oil.

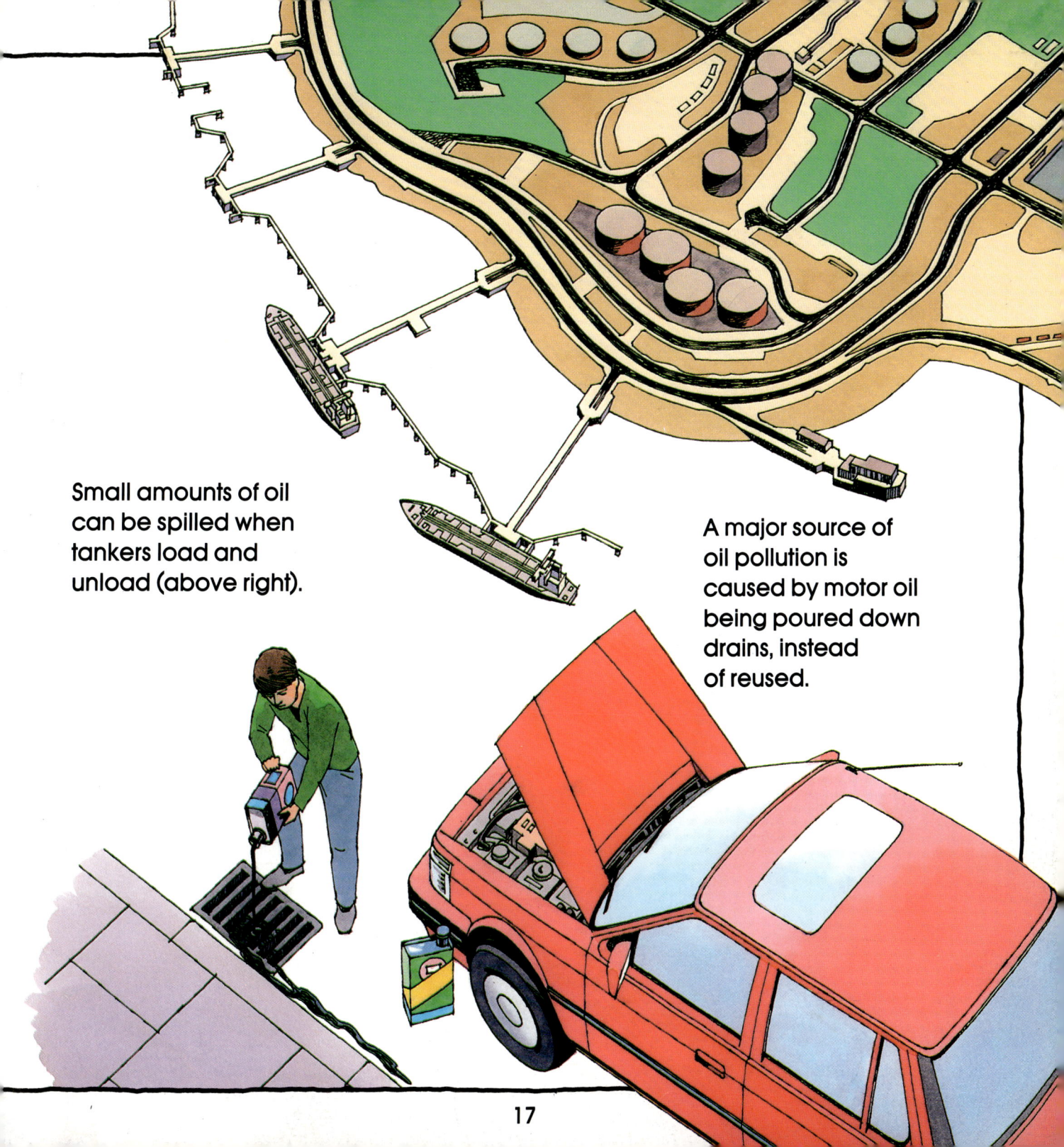

Small amounts of oil can be spilled when tankers load and unload (above right).

A major source of oil pollution is caused by motor oil being poured down drains, instead of reused.

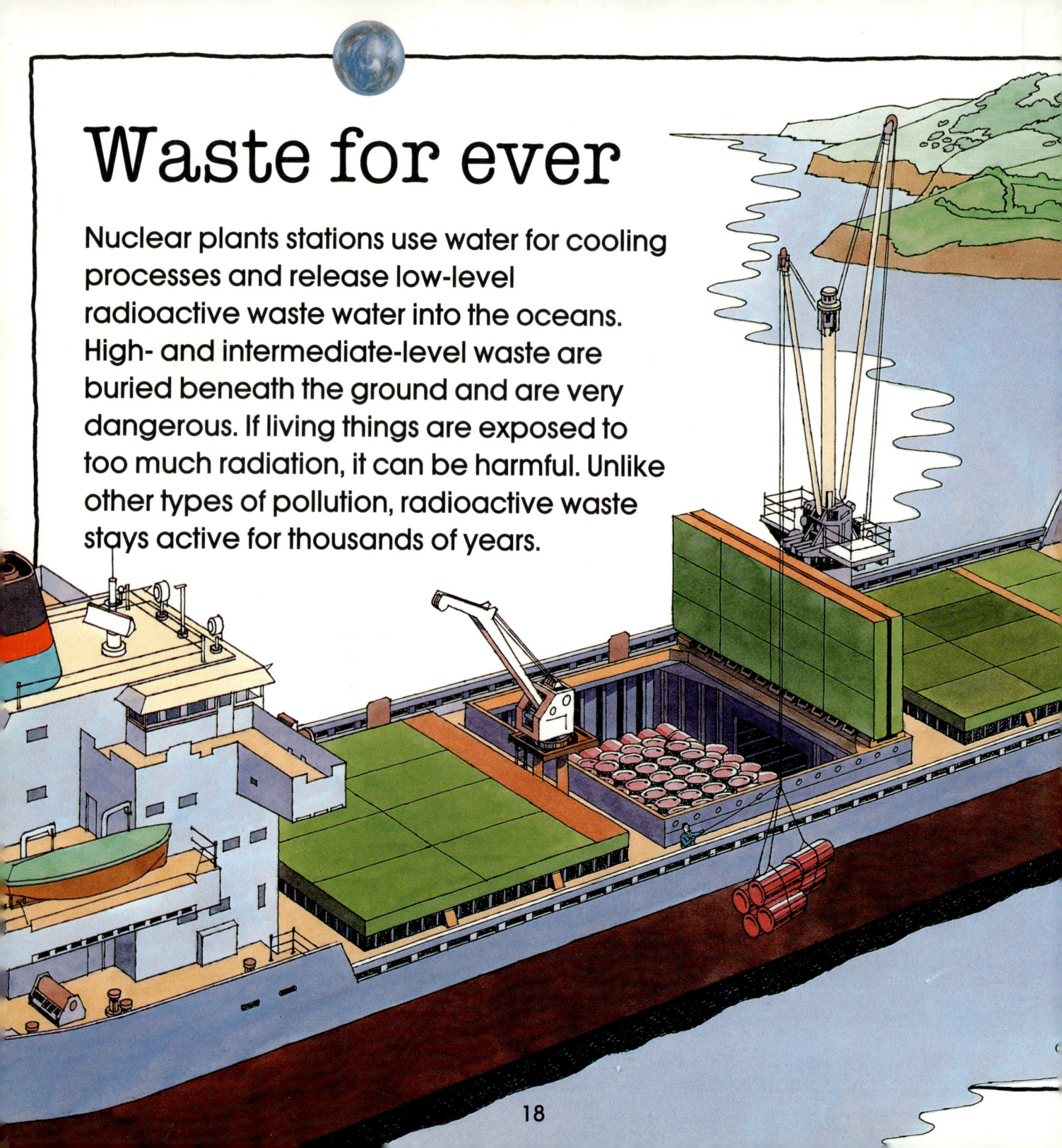

Waste for ever

Nuclear plants stations use water for cooling processes and release low-level radioactive waste water into the oceans. High- and intermediate-level waste are buried beneath the ground and are very dangerous. If living things are exposed to too much radiation, it can be harmful. Unlike other types of pollution, radioactive waste stays active for thousands of years.

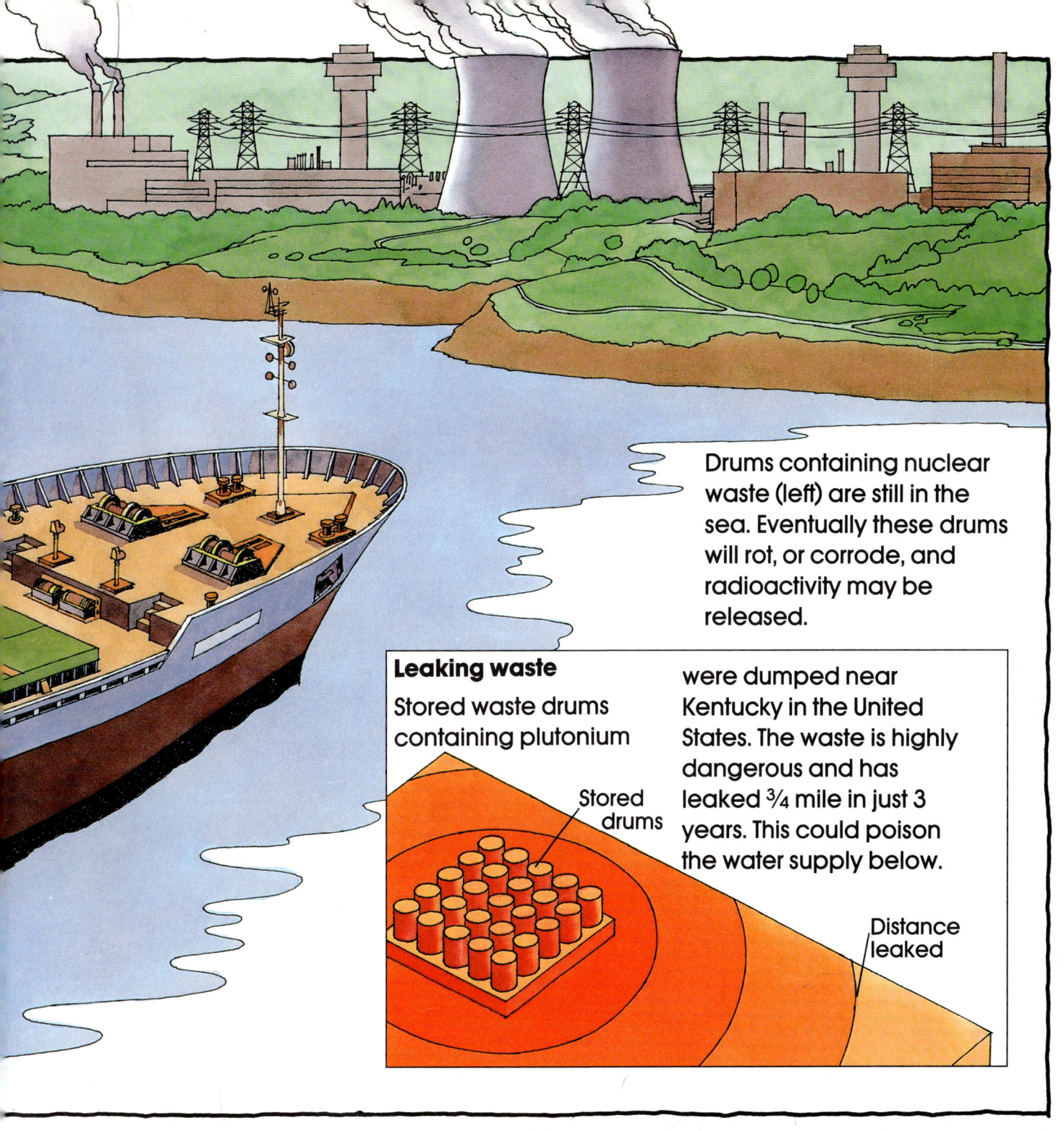

Drums containing nuclear waste (left) are still in the sea. Eventually these drums will rot, or corrode, and radioactivity may be released.

Leaking waste

Stored waste drums containing plutonium were dumped near Kentucky in the United States. The waste is highly dangerous and has leaked ¾ mile in just 3 years. This could poison the water supply below.

Weakened by the effects of pollution, many seals become ill. During long periods of warm weather when seals come together to breed, diseases quickly spread.

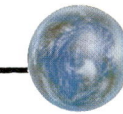

Causing disease

Pollution can seriously affect the health of both people and animals. At Minamata in Japan, mercury pollution from a factory got into the sea. Fish poisoned by the mercury were eaten by local people, with terrible results. Many suffered from nervous diseases and at least 43 people died. Fertilizer pollution in Louisiana has killed much of the wildlife that once lived on the coast there.

Many seals in the Baltic Sea have terrible sores and parts of their bodies are deformed as a result of chemical pollution.

Flatfish cancer
Near the mouths of badly polluted rivers, flatfish like plaice can develop cancers.

Hot spots

In Britain, the nuclear processing plant Sellafield pumps water containing small amounts of radioactivity into the Irish Sea, which is thought to be the most contaminated sea in the world. The Gulf and the Caribbean are two of the world's busiest oil routes and suffer most from oil pollution. Both the North Sea and the Mediterranean are affected by vast amounts of sewage from towns on their coasts.

The map shows which oceans are most affected by pollution. The worst areas are those with a lot of industry (shown in pink).

Atlantic Ocean

Pacific Ocean

Whales and dolphins often pass through severely polluted areas and may become ill or even die as a result.

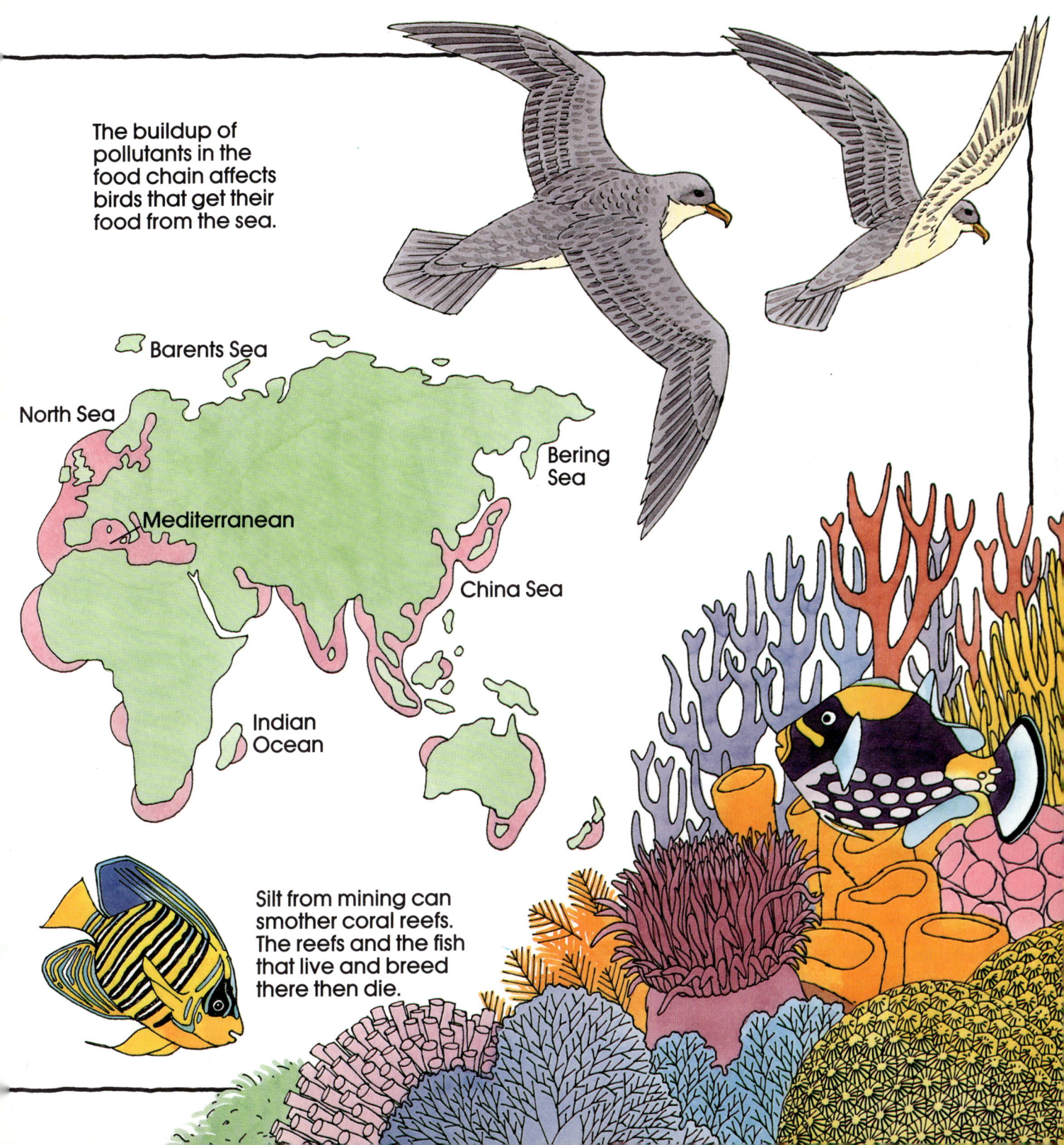

Cleaning up

People from countries all over the world are now realizing the importance of cleaning up the oceans. Strong laws on pollution must be passed and enforced by governments all over the world. Certain pollutants should be banned until their effects on the environment are fully known. And where possible, attempts should be made to recycle all kinds of wastes.

Below are some of the most common ways the sea is polluted, and the action being taken to stop this pollution.

Some countries have now banned the dumping of domestic rubbish under the London Dumping Convention of 1972.

Undersea pipelines still leak waste into the sea. No action has been taken to reduce this yet.

Burning British waste at sea is to be stopped by the end of 1991.

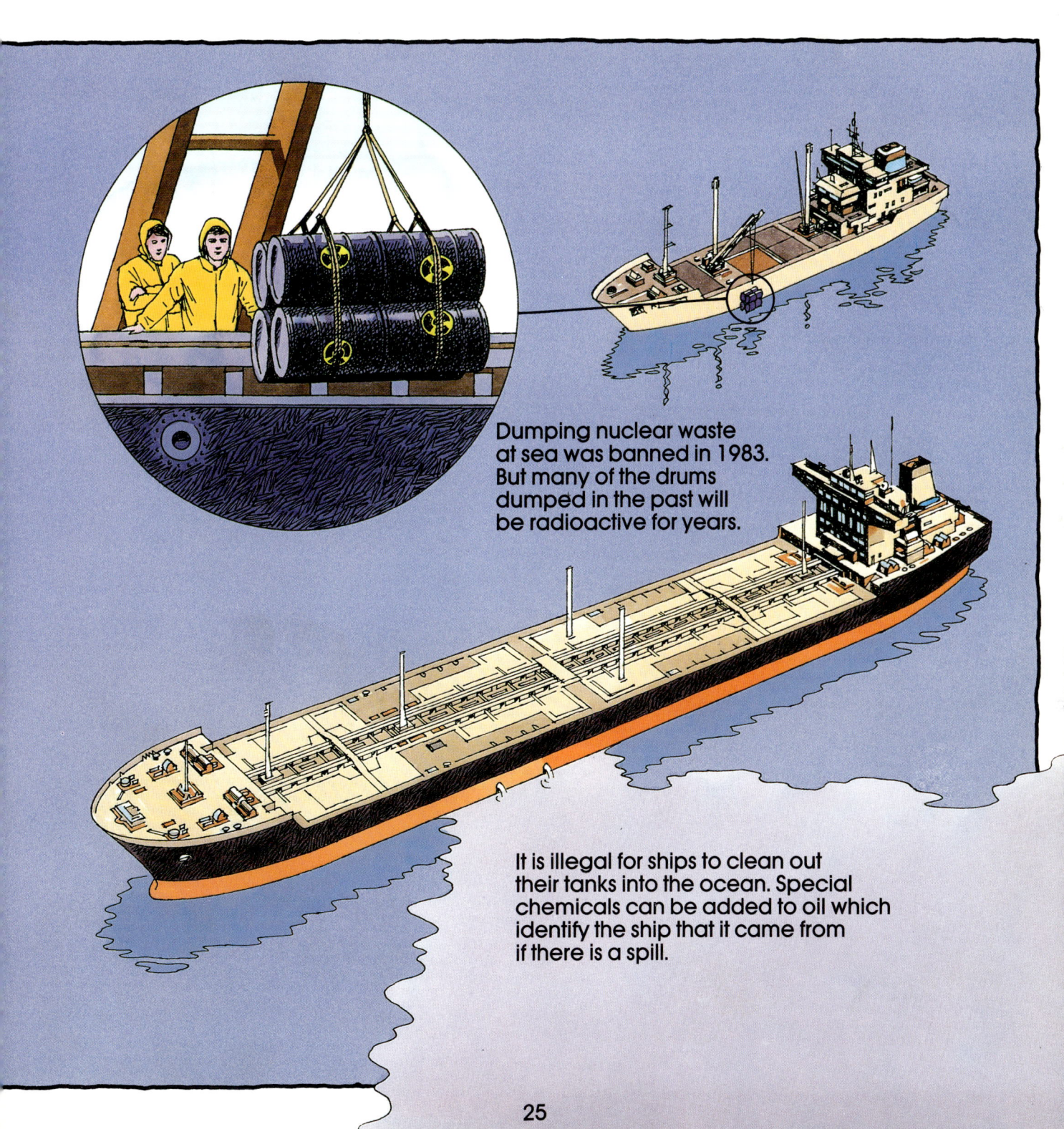

Taking action

In 1991 the North Sea Conference agreed that the dumping of sewage should be banned by 1998. Burning British waste at sea must also be stopped by the end of 1991, and the dumping of liquid industrial waste becomes illegal after 1992. These and other measures must be taken to stop the dumping of all pollutants, and to clean up the oceans worldwide.

It is people who pollute the oceans. So it is our responsibility to clean them up. Public protests can make people more aware of the problem, and force governments to take decisive action.

In some areas, ocean patrols have been introduced to check for any new cases of pollution and reduce the damage that may be caused.

Did you know?

Mangrove swamps, shown below, are home to many different kinds of animals which may suffer if the swamps are polluted. At Bimini in the Bahamas, lemon sharks leave their pups in the mangroves. The pups hide and feed there. But if the mangroves are destroyed, the sharks may disappear, too.

A large oil spill in the Arctic or Antarctic could be disastrous. An oil slick creeps under the ice and becomes trapped there. The dark patches take in, or absorb, heat, and the ice melts. This could change the temperatures locally and even influence the weather in other parts of the planet.

Until recently, millions of drums of highly toxic and radioactive wastes were dumped into the ocean. The deep sea was thought to be calm, but now we know it is not. Gigantic storms rage on the seabed and last for weeks. These storms could damage the drums, possibly causing them to leak.

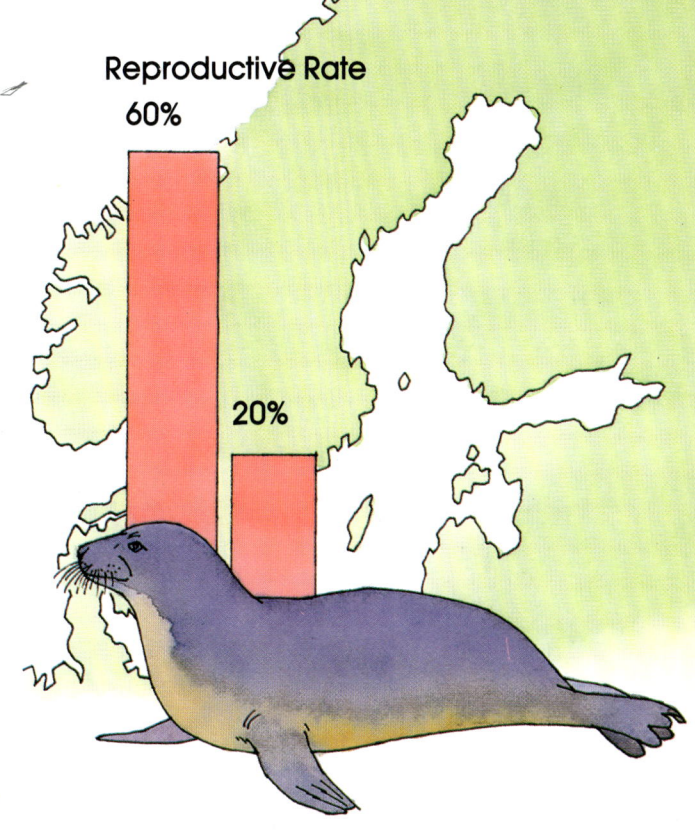

Wildlife in and around the Baltic Sea is being harmed by the huge amounts of fertilisers and industrial pollution that end up there. Chemicals called PCBs, which are used in the electrical industry, can make animals infertile, which means they cannot breed, or develop deformed beaks or wings.

The Mediterranean is almost completely surrounded by land. It has no tide, so if pollution gets into the sea, it can stay there for many years. Many towns and factories along its coast release sewage and other wastes into the sea, and tar balls, a form of oil pollution, are found floating in the water.

Mediterranean Sea

In the past, fishermen only caught as many fish as they needed, leaving plenty behind to breed for the future. Today, however, many fishermen use drift nets. These "walls of death" trap and kill anything that swims into them. Exploiting the sea's resources in this way has led to the decline of many species.

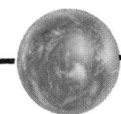

Glossary

Algal bloom
Too much plant food from fertilizers in the sea makes algae grow very fast or "bloom." When the algae die, they use up all the oxygen in the water.

Fertilizers
Chemicals that farmers put on crops to make them grow.

Food chain
A chain of plants and animals that depend upon each other for food. If one stage of the chain is affected by pollution, the whole chain can suffer.

PCBs (Polychlorinated biphenyls)
Chemicals used in the electrical industry. When they enter an ocean food chain they are very dangerous. They can cause terrible deformities in seals and deaths in seabirds. PCBs break down very slowly in the environment, and can remain in food chains for years.

Radioactive waste
The waste from nuclear reactors and other nuclear processes. High-level waste includes the most dangerous substances, like plutonium, which is harmful for thousands of years. Low-level waste includes materials that come into direct contact with radioactive substances, such as a plant worker's overalls.

Toxic waste
These are the wastes from industry that are poisonous to plants and animals.

Index

A
algae 9, 19, 31

C
chemical waste 10, 11, 13, 24, 26, 29
coral reefs 18, 19, 23

D
DDT 11
disease 20, 21, 30
dumping 13, 14, 16, 17, 24-46

F
factories 10, 11, 14, 21, 29
fertilizers 9, 21, 29, 31
food chain 4, 5, 8-10, 31

L
land waste 17, 18

M
metals 7, 21, 30

N
nuclear waste 16-17, 24-25, 29, 31

O
oil spills 7, 14, 15, 24, 25, 28

P
PCBs 29, 31
pesticides 8, 9
plankton 4, 5, 9, 21
poisons 8, 9, 13, 18

R
radioactivity 16-17, 31
rubbish 12, 13, 24

S
sewage 11, 12, 19, 24, 26
silt 18, 19, 23

T
toxic waste 24, 29, 31